Spine

spine

K. I. PRESS

GASPEREAU PRESS PRINTERS & PUBLISHERS MMIV

to Adam

CONTENTS

What Are Little Girls Made Of?

WHAT ARE LITTLE GIRLS MADE OF?

We are serpents, eyes shining through the dark, not yet
nearsighted with age. Slithering in water, land, or air, we are
amphibious with wings, tall as mirrored buildings, look into us.
We steal the eggs of old men,
wizards, knights, panderers, and kings,
lunatics, prisoners, absent-minded professors,
the man standing on the corner preaching
with his hat to the crowd. We steal all
that is round,
seeds, coins, Hula Hoops,
all manner of fruit.

We are giraffes, how easy it is
to lose our heads, for our heads
to lose our bodies, how easy
to reach all manner of fruit,
grazing in trees on roofs
of mirrored office buildings, gazing
at little invisible men
working away and looking out
in horror—

We are Queen Kong,
we will leave you
falling out of saddles,
losing track of your hair.

Buy us a present. Tell us a story.

MADNESS

How easily they go mad in books, sport rare deformities.
How boring to read of lives unmarred
by homicidal wives and hunchbacked uncles.
How slippery the slope. How the woman in the dirty cloak
raves, how she burns
the house down.

How unfortunate the pretty girls lapsed into hysterics.
How mysterious the mute in the orchard, the blind man
in the castle. How the good old madwoman
is mad mad mad how

nurses roll up their sleeves
and doctors shake their heads.
How Lady Macbeth flits about.
How full the sanatorium. How the consumptives
can't straighten their backs and the cripples
take to coughing fits. How hidden
children and wives are kept

in their rooms
reading books about wives
kept in their rooms reading
books about girls reading books
in their rooms about fires
burning them down.

SCIENCE FICTION

I was not found in the cabbage patch, I walked
out of a spaceship. If I try hard enough and wave and blink,
doors will close, and puppets move
without their masters.
Can you hear me thinking? Mom?

MOM! Tell me where I came from, really, this time.
Let's run away together and be quiet.
Let me live on another planet.
It's space. There's room there.

FRECKLES

Only five Catholic girls born in town that year.
They must have lived lives
out of one of my books. I had to find which one.
They had touched horses, weren't afraid of dogs, complained,
proud, when bundled off to doctors for bee stings.

They couldn't spell much, but they knew how to drive. The sun
aggravated their freckles. They told stories

not in my books, who touched whom where,
getting laid in tents. They didn't like ghost stories
but knew good threats and words I didn't.

My only friends. I imagined
they were books. Censored. Ending abruptly.

CONSUMPTION

"… don't let her read books until she gets more spring in her step."

"I guess that's why I'm so thin—I am dreadful thin, ain't I? There isn't a pick on my bones. I do love to imagine I'm nice and plump, with dimples in my elbows."

—ANNE OF GREEN GABLES

I .

Fair girls are in danger
of fainting dead away,
shriveling in the nights,
sunken eyes, sheets barely
ruffled.

They tried to teach me
reading could kill.
They lied.

I could consume all the books
and still have room,

stay indoors squinting,
hunched beside candles.

If those teachers were girls
they would douse themselves
in something flammable,
stay away from candles, say
well, that's all we can do:

can't read
in the dark.

The pale girls,
good martyrs,
good philosophers,
smile themselves gently away;

even the rosy-cheeked girls,
too full of life,
die by arrangement, right
on time
on wedding days.

There is a spring in me
but not in my step
and I am not sorry for it,
I am not sorry.
I cannot stay.

2.

Laptop, lamp off.

I read dark words
the surface shining like
candles, emitting whatever
radiation it desires.

The sneaking suspicion they were right.
What did I learn
that did not disappoint.

I changed my mind.
Will you marry me, leave me
with a lamp,
alone?

3.

At Lowood School
the girls form thin lines,
hold out hands
for burnt porridge.

Their stockings hang in folds,
their cheekbones, their hair
pulled tight.

At another school
the girls form thin lines,
vomit in the bathroom stalls,
hair pulled back against their skulls.

4.

Somewhere today
flames are burning
girls alive, somewhere books
are burning again.

Somewhere a child
does not come out alive.
Somewhere is Green Gables,
everywhere is Gateshead.

Somewhere a girl is wasting dead away
because there is not a pick on her bones,
because she has stopped
consuming.

The odds vary.
The flames are the same.

5.

Look at books
and love them, sadly

seeing why we loved them
then.

ANNE AND JANE

Anne

Every day before I went to school
I would weep in the outhouse.
I would weep in my bed every night
after turning down the lamp.
I would weep when I walked
with lunches and leather-bound
prayers and equations. Every
ugly grey and serviceable
thing about me. Every freckled
toad. Every cake
that fell.

And everyone called it
daydreaming and invented
exercises to rein
my ways of thinking. As if retreat
was not deliberate and this
mucking about with flash-
cards and electrodes would somehow
make me happy.

They should have hooked
the machine to the whole world
to jump-start it. Instead I wept
my huge, real tears
and they evaporated with mathematical precision.

Jane

I thought if I were given a second chance,
a second time to confront not only him
but the whole gang of them,
with my wits about me this time, I would
cut off his balls and kick
the bitch down the stairs. Idle fantasy,
but as I approached the grounds I was not at all worried
about my plan—merely its unoriginality.
How brute I would look.

And so when I saw the charred remains
my heart fell all the storeys from that same tower,
the resolve knocked out of it. There is nothing worse
than seeing your enemies defeated in spectacular manner
before you've had time to spit out goodbye.

I followed his trail because again
I had not my wits about me. I no longer had
any idea what I would do or say and so
I walked straight into another one of his traps,
his and God's, for they were in
some kind of nasty cahoots,
a trap which nullified my newest trick—
impressiveness and finery and the huge
black coach awaiting the smallest movement
of my small, small wrist.

So not only my resolve, but all of me,
fell again and again, victim

to compassion. I cannot count
all the women I have seen cut down this way.
It wears you down over the years
until you can't even remember
that you hate them. Your cursing
directed at your own self. Exactly
the way they had planned.

   Anne

He always claimed he knew he'd marry me
the day I gave him
two black eyes and broke
his nose. To this day I don't know
why I did. But I am still
regretting it,

sitting here rocking, with children
fighting wars and drowning in wells. I listen
to echoes, to babies gurgling
in the clouds. And then it rains
and the light changes.
Thousands of tiny hands
gesture at me.

I am almost
alone. I wish I were
alone. Every ghost has descended
upon my rocking chair and every
single one knows who I am.

He died
and brought the whole underworld
into my parlour.

Jane

At first I delighted in torturing him.
He was blind and I thought it was funny,
moving his water 'round the table, hiding keys,
letting him walk around with shit on his forehead, which I put there,
an emblem of repentance. His dead eyes. He couldn't even
cry. Called my name. Maybe he thought
there was another one of me
doing these things, the elf who bewitched
his horse. I killed his dog
and bore him a child.
I let the boy run wild, although
I could have bought him anything. His little face
obliterated by dirt and the scratches
of brambles and unruly cats.
I loved him.

It turned out the blind man was hiding
his sight from me a little more
each day. Were we not
a happy pair. He feared
if he could see, I would leave him
and take the boy, who in any case
seemed to pay him little attention. I suspected
nothing until the day

I was washing my hair
and felt his eyes on me.

   Anne

Sometimes I think maybe I was happy
for a very long time. The kind of happiness
that covers you
like an eggshell.

   Jane

Mended.

   Anne

With beeswax. Crazy
glue oozing from my pores. Flies
stuck to me, and I would
smile, smile, smile, smile, smile.

   Jane

I took what I needed and like I said
bore his child
a son with black hair but no brooding
yet. For a while I thought
I could kill him too but again this seemed
so already done.

23

Anne

I read it in school.

Jane

So did I. It is hard
to be new. I expected
of myself great newness:
new ways of thinking,
of dealing with rats,
and burning things.

Anne

I would darn socks with the wrong colour yarn
and think I was clever.

Jane

We both deceived ourselves. I found
newness, it is true, every day a new
reason to stay there, a new reason
to let the boy live. I taught him
a little. He was good
at math. He counted
matches compulsively and the steps
leading up to the attic and the few words
his father would utter on a given day.

Then he multiplied these things using
a formula he invented himself and came to me
with the answer I had been waiting for.

Leave him. Take me with you.
He can see you,
he can see the oily glint in your eyes, leave before
he cuts you out somehow.
Take me with you. Meet your black coach
in town before he realizes
what is happening. You owe him nothing.
You never married him.

You're a tramp.

Anne

But I never once thought of leaving. Never once.
I thought: what else could I want? I didn't remember
my hard-living days, my need for the world
to wake up to me.

My children were mostly clever in a kind
of bland smiling way, like how
a clever dog learns to please its master. Blithe
and undemanding, like their father.
Not clever enough to avoid certain things.
Too dutiful for their own good.
Some of them received in their genes
a certain weeping melancholy, but untempered
by any longing for knowledge.

By any longing at all, as far
as I could tell.

Did I teach them that?
I had lived on an island for so long
I didn't think beyond the water.
Then there was a war
and my sons disappeared.
Then a daughter, heartbroken, thought
she was Jesus one day
and walked out into the sea.
Another went to Boston
to live in a flat with a man and a fur coat
and I never heard from her again.
Another died giving birth.

And we sat here in our rocking chairs
and looked out the window and I darned
socks as he watched the lighthouse
and smoked his pipe.

  Jane

A few last things
kept me back. Some days I remembered the gazebo
where I kissed him in the most inappropriate manner
and later with my small inelegant luggage
sat in grim resolve. It might still be standing.
It is always those few still-standing things
that misdirect hope. That gazebo
was my memory of passion, the hope

that I still loved him,
or still hated him,
and could leave again.

I think you wanted to love your family
as much as I wanted to hate mine.
But we are not allowed anything
so pure. We must
just make do.

  Anne

I never wept when my family
was gone. I forgot I ever had.
The dead flies began
to fall from my eggshell
and crumble to dust. Soon
I would be naked again as the day
I ran across a neighbouring farmer's field
and they caught me and tied me
to my bed for fear
I loved nature.

  Jane

The trick was he had taken my hatred
and replaced it with nothing.
The trick was all I had to suck
into the vacuum was my son.
I looked at him with shame

27

and it was shame I sucked inside me
when I turned my back on him
as he betrayed me, screaming bloody murder
and calling me whore. His father
had been feeding him secret
sugar sandwiches. They will rot you.
Sharp shards of sweet ground glass.
Pretending at love rots you harder
than hatred or bitterness
because it makes you hate them
and hate yourself
and hate love
and hate hatred.
And what else is left?

Anne

I wouldn't be surprised if that little boy
made it to the city, eventually,
beating women, starving dogs and being
very, very cruel to his horse.

As for me, it took years and years for all the smiles and flies
to fall off. Maybe, I thought,
I could give him
two black eyes again.

Jane

You killed him then?

Anne

Oh, no. He died in his sleep. He was 62,
the town doctor, they gave me
a pension and I am now the old woman
whose overgrown yard scares children
away. Little do they know
I sit here terrorized
by babies' hands,
hands I never wanted
in the first place.

GENTLEMAN

All their class held these principles: I supposed, then, they had
reasons for holding them, such as I could not fathom. It seemed
to me that, were I a gentleman like him, I would take to my bosom
only such a wife as I could love ...

—JANE EYRE

Were I a gentleman, I would learn to tap dance,
don cotton gloves to handle antique
kitchenware, arrowheads and dinosaur bones.

Were I a gentleman, first I would comb
remote corners for certain wet, shining pebbles.
I might have to watch them shrivel.
I might keep them in a jam-jar.

Were I a gentleman, I would not sit
idle and wait for eagles to storm my fields of sheep
or precipitate on my battlements.

I might dress myself as a scarecrow, run
circles round the house, and roar.
I would be more than lord and master.

I would be rugged, not follow.
I would send for what gave me pleasure
and drink it, despite whispers
from the gallery.
I would love flowers.
I would not collect china-dolls, nor stare into mirrors
or picture-windows. I would act.
I would hold out my hands.

SLUSH PILE

Wanted: powerful white men
who always wanted
to be writers. Sense of
relentlessness required. Demanding
phone manner preferred.

It is an advantage to be writing
a thriller about white-collar criminals
and Colombian drug money. The novel
should be set in Toronto,
Vancouver, Los Angeles, London, Paris, Cairo
and the jungles of the Amazon. You will need
at least one action scene on a boat, with sex.
The sex should be violent.

Preference will be given
to candidates who have sat
on the Ontario Securities Commission
or the board of a major financial institution.
The ideal candidate
will have served briefly as an MP
in the eighties.

If you are on top of your game, have finally
completed that chef-d'œuvre
you have been working on for the past sixteen years, then
this position is for you.

Wanted: men who are used
to getting what they want and really
only wanted to be writers.

Advance commensurate
with the size of your manuscript.

Serious applicants only.

THREE ROSE GARDEN VARIATIONS

1. Innocence

Does innocence preclude the act of reading?

You are not a roll of film. Don't blink

those eyes, it doesn't fool
anyone, children

shoot each other, themselves, you
blame oil tankers or slasher films,
death by exposure
to words and pictures, who can be bothered,
it's so easy

ignoring sharp pains
in your leg, a lump, sudden
bruises.

You would like to think
a warning appears, the text
upside-down in the mirror.

The space below
bridges, trains,
does not tell, contains
no real messages.
There is nothing
between the lines
that you didn't put there.

2. *Land of Oz*

The writer just needs to write, and the reader, if she is a good
reader, will find herself in it. The text will be the land of Oz.

When I entered, I was foxtail
ditch thistle, clover dot, pollen
mote, airborne
flailing
        then
centripetal.

Felt the grass there
under hard soles, and knew it wasn't common
grass, my grass, sky not
my sky, too
full of creatures,
large grains of earth, so ready
to succumb to gravity.

My blades, the burrs I used
to shoot at trespassers, fell.

I was inside and that was enough.
Giants might pick me and place me
on the backs of flying toads, and princesses might threaten
to sever my head, but okay:
who needs a body here, I could roll my eyes
across the green grass all day
become a field of poppies
dream a thousand bodies
to enter.

3. Not Difficult

She reads not because she wishes to, but because she has to.
It is necessary. She either reads or dies.

No one ever said
it was not difficult. Trapped and reading
in a burning building. Or the burning
bush. Timber toppling, pages blackened
beyond ink. You hold your book
to your chest afraid to move it
from the safety of your body.

No one said
it would not be difficult
to keep reading through every age they make you
run through, thistles and twigs that snap
across your legs. The point of the matter.
You hold your books tightly
wound together with old string, covers
yellow with tape.

Looking for some word
that will save your life.
You might not remember
the words after you've seen them.
The point of the matter.
You are reading for your life.

Because somewhere others like you
are coagulating out of nuclear goo, descending
to earth from the planet with two suns. If you met them
you could read their minds. And then some.

No one ever said
it's not difficult reading minds,
even your own,
while explosions come up from underground,
while you live in a minefield
and who doesn't. Just try
crossing the street
nose in a book.

No one said
it would not be difficult
when the lights aren't on.

The Immaculate Conception

THE IMMACULATE CONCEPTION

Hell was covered up
in yards of purple silk
and pussy willows; it smelled
faintly of rosewater.

It was elementary school and it was
a soft sell. Just a second skin
ever so slowly petrifying
until one day you noticed
an uncomfortable stone shell
constricting your movement.

*

Like a Virgin
was the talk of the schoolyard.
The same year friends began
admitting to hand jobs. Incidents
in pickup trucks increased. We promised
we'd never breathe a word, and didn't. Things
just got worse from there.

The chastity speakers came. A woman named
The Chastitute passed dice around
the room and said
condoms break.
If your number comes up
you are pregnant, HIV-positive,
a great temptation to abortion doctors.

You can turn back the clock, become
a born-again virgin. If you stop now.
If you break it up. If you admit
you started it.

*

Even way up here,
I suffocate with men
on top of me.
So much fuss and trouble.

Surrender
or the nunnery. Very Ophelia.

I concentrate on known quantities, on what is stable,
and written, and will not bite me, and will not wreck
the sheets; will not ask me to leave
and come back when I am able to compose myself.

I was reading a book, I was reading The Name of the Rose,
I was reading Paul, and Augustine.
I was reading Ted Hughes. I read
on my back or front or sometimes side, I read slowly
sometimes and quickly too, and slowly again.
I stopped and started and languished and slept
and woke and started to read again.

It was Christmas vacation, I could sleep in, and did,
I would roll over, open my eyes, and smile
at the growing congregation of books
across the bed.

　*

The Virgin Mary, in her bedchamber, again
and again. The light is too bright,
she is squinting.
Her number is up. She looked up
from her book, didn't she, she stopped
paying strict attention. There's
an angel standing there—now
she's fucked.

JOANNA

I have come into my garden, my sister, my bride;
I have gathered my myrrh with my spice.
I have eaten my honeycomb and my honey.

Father is laid up with leeches, the doctor
empties his blood and piss in pans
in the pasture. Petra found him
in the courtyard. He asked her
for his name.

Father is laid up with Mother
knitting, the priest laying
hands, Father keeping his
folded, to himself, wondering
where he is and who these people are
with their busy hands. Capable of
the finest work, precision, pleasure,
his hands rest, awkward. I've never seen them
still before.

They took his clothes off
to drain him; among
the bites and blisters his penis lies
sideways, and suddenly so small.
It was always so loved,
and charted in his books.

*

You've been working
too hard, too hard. Father,
I know everything and nothing
about you. Stone, stone, stone.
Fuck, fuck, fuck.

Daughters and business partners,
mistresses and models, all eating
apples, skin
glowing in firelight. Listening
to your incantations, your spells and diatribes.
So many laughing Ariels. Multiple
Mirandas. But the Calibans
you didn't carve.

I can't remember the first time
I took my clothes off.
I would play in the studio, banging away
at my own little nude block of stone. I made
very little progress with my stone, and then
you'd ask me to stop and lie this way or that
for your sketchbook. My eyes so wide.

My sisters remember things
somewhat differently. You never drew me
in quite the same way. Not
the same way at all.

In the chapel I confessed
to fictions. Why can't we all

be part of you, flesh
of your flesh, chips off your own stones?

*

Before Petra called me, this morning,
I was planning my wedding.
This afternoon I sat in the press room.
You loved me less
and to compensate you drew me a face,
a face only a typographer could love.
Eccentric, someone said. I don't know what he meant.

You always told me I was beautiful,
that you loved my hair, my stomach, my eyes;
you always embraced me with such pride,
declared I smelled of honey, told me
how to wear my hair, my clothes.
You named me. I am Joan.
I hear God, and I hear you.
I won't marry him if you don't want me to.

Just stop pretending you don't know my name!
I am Joan. I did everything you wanted.
When the village children threw stones at me.
When Mother took my hand
and led me away from your workshop. When my sisters
conspired and laughed about how you had touched them.
I did everything you wanted and you kept away.
I would have done anything but you never asked.
I am your mission, lost without you.

We have a young sister,
and her breasts are not yet grown.
What shall we do for our sister
for the day she is spoken for?
If she is a wall,
we will build towers of silver on her.
If she is a door,
we will enclose her with panels of cedar.

THE LETTERS

1. *To the Church at Thessalonica*

They made fun of me
in Philippi, and in Corinth
they shook their private parts
and laughed.
But with you I could be myself,
without trickery or promises. You will remember
how well I behaved, no bribe attempts,
no inky stories of the underworld. I could tell
the truth, no shadowing things
in mythology or rhyme.

It's not my fault I haven't returned.
Satan sent crises of mind, spirit and weather,
forgetfulness of the feet, and eyes
shutting every night, burying hours
in blackness. I tried
to stay awake, to walk and swim and ride to you,
but these devils caught me and bound me by the ankles.
Still each night my mind races
to find you before the moon
reaches your side of the planet.

If we never see each other again, the Lord will help us
prove our love. It will grow like acorns
and burst through the clouds.
A forest to fill the deserts
and the seas.

*

There are sleeping men,
there are weeping women.
Without hope, these things happen.
Do not cry, crying
is passion: even when they pull you
apart by your limbs, keep a straight face.
I am here, I am still alive, and I am
awake. They will never catch me
napping. Sleep is a portal.
I don't like what I see there, sometimes.
Ropes, and snakes turning into ropes.
Wheels, and rocks turning into wheels.
Pigheads and lopped-off feet.
Black blood bursting through
my skin. My captors turning
to fire and jumping
from mountaintops and raining down on me.

I have been awake now for 13 days.
It helps that my mind
races always toward you.
It has not seen you for so long.

Dreams are portals. We should not pass through.
Sometimes at night, you might see angels.
Those are not dreams, but true angels.
You must stay awake
to have such visions, stay awake as long as you can.
Keep a noisy dog, a cold stone always beneath you.
Keep watch.
Your eyes fixed
on the air.

Sleep is a rat.
Keep watch on it.

God is a murderer
entering your home with a knife.
He will tie you up
and cut your heart out
if you are sleeping,
and feed it to His dog,
the devil. If you are awake,

He will still cut your heart out,
but carry it carefully with Him, and let you follow Him
out the door and into the morning.
I've said this before.
He carries a light with Him
and a scalpel, and never sleeps.
So listen: do not sleep. Keep watch
with me, become crickets.
A chorus, waiting.

2. *To the Church at Corinth* (i)

Words in this world
have no meaning.
Rights and wrongs do not come
leaping from throats.
I know God
will cut my heart out and open with
no science or anaesthetic.
Under sharp lights. Every one of you, the saved
and the lost, and the angels too, hovering

like giant hummingbirds,
will gather round the table to hiss and holler.
An auditorium of hatred.
Such is life, eyes and ears and chest wide open, for an apostle like me.

I will ruin Corinth.
I will ruin all Greece.

Just say the word and someone
will show up with an axe.

*

It is hard to save you
from each other: you can't keep your hands to yourselves.
You should touch your wives,
if you must, instead of chasing sheep, or doing it
for Aphrodite on the hill.

There goes my seed,
spreading its message across the world.
I have become everything:

weak, strong, drunk, sober,
full of beans and straight ahead,
over the moon and under the weather,
like an elephant and like a camel.
Like a lonely teardrop
and the teeth of an angry clown.
I am the man
with heads in all dimensions.

*

My ancestors lived under the cloud
that passed through the sea. They lived
in mist and every moment
baptized them a million times.
They drank from rock
and though it was the same rock
we drink from now, God
littered deserts with their dead.

If you do not do
what I tell you to do, you will be killed
by snakes.

That's a warning.
Do not ask me to explain myself again.
Shut up and cut your hair,
or put a hat on,
as befits your genitals. We've always dealt with hair this way
in our church.

Certainly, everyone's gift is different.
The Holy Spirit is like a box of chocolates:

wisdom
faith
healing
palm reading
the ability to tell a hawk from a henhouse
speaking in tongues
omigash rickshawf marigelicant omdinim
habanasheroup robewubvhiv
marigelicant voo

But even so.
The foot does not say:
     I'm going to grow whiskers and open a vaudeville show
in Arkansas.
The head does not say:
     Fuck you.
The ears do not say:
     No one can tell me
     what to hear and understand.
The tongue does not say:
     I can speak freely.

I say: Fuck you, foot and eyes and mouth,
if you say these things.

We are one body and must move
with a body's purpose.
We may not be much to look at,
but we can smell
dissent, ferret it out
and chop it off.

When I was young in Tarsus,
I would draw
on my skin with pens and think.
I had time
to walk in gardens just because
I loved to walk in gardens
and lie in grass just because
I loved to lie in grass.
I wanted for nothing
and would tell people
I loved them.

I have stopped these things,
now that I am a man.

3. *To the Church at Corinth* (ii)

I am out of my mind.
You refuse me

from indifference, or spite, or whim,
or the influence of influential men.
But there are more of my words in you
than in any letter I could write. Your hearts
may be stone but you cannot erase what is etched there.

Whenever they lash me for heresy,
each stroke puts me further
into your cells. I have endured

shipwrecks and wild beasts with many fangs,
evil curses, ignorance,
smart-alecks and leeches. I have been lynched
and trampled and beaten and kicked in the groin.
I have been stoned more than once,
robbed many times, spit upon daily, stripped of my clothes,
set adrift in a leaky boat, thrown in a pit
with snakes. Through all of this I count myself
lucky to have known you.

I won't take it back. It
was necessary and true. I will not lose you
to magicians who dish

freedom out in ladles, send you running
back to your brothels and temples,
blood and ashes. Come back.

4. *To the Church at Galatia*

I wish they would just
have done with it
and castrate themselves.

You may shave your heads, walk bare-
foot in coals, sting yourselves with bees,
but if your hearts are not stung,
you have nothing.

Instead, let us follow
the new diet: "What Would Jesus Eat?"
Jesus would eat
whatever you can find in a Lebanese restaurant.
I mean it. The whole buffet.

I was dying when we first met, almost
blind. Had you been surgeons,
you each would have sewn
your own eyes
into my sockets.
I would have seen
many times over,
like a bug. In all directions.

Do not suffer
for your own sakes. Suffer
for ours. If you offer up
your hands, eyes, tentacles, very
atoms, you will be part of us.
Never alone, forever awake,
whoever you are.

Woman, man, sheep, goat, surgeon, apostle, bug:
you will be melded into one large, magnificent creature,
breathing fire and scaled with gold,
guarding jealously
the whole world.

5. *To the Church at Philippi*

In these, the last days,
you are searchlights. When God comes,
the Fourth of July.
I am tempted
to die. I cannot wait
for the world to end.

I am tired. I want to join
the angels and vampires.
I want to find heaven in my sleep,
and drop gently down to earth again
each day. But if I sleep

I see only dogs, their mouths wide, and snakes,
glowing. Sometimes long caravans
walking slowly on the bottom of the sea.

In this, the end of days, the wicked
are enjoying themselves immensely. They are implosions
sucking everything
into darkness. Searchlights, I want to see

your bright cylinders reaching
the sky outside my jail room. You
are the best church. Better
than the Thessalonians. Your package
smelled lonely, and of the Lord.

   6. *Dear Philemon*

Many in Ephesus speak of you.
Your white home, and stables,
and servants overflowing
from the kitchen into the halls.

Your boy Onesimus
is here. Your large hands and closed stables.
He has offered his soul
to my chains, and carries with him
all my energy
and thoughts.

I think they will let me
go soon. I have taken all his sins
upon me, and will set out
as burdened with evil
as I ever was
heading for Damascus.
I will go to Corinth, and then to Rome.

I will stop
and visit you.
Have all your wickedness
ready.

7. *To the Church at Rome*

We have met before, in visions. Rome is beautiful,
and from it we will conquer the earth. Soon
my day in Rome will come.
Leave room for me.

*

What manner of sinners
do you have in Rome? They must be
grand ones. I have seen much wickedness
and cannot be deceived.
I have seen people
worship crocodiles! And snakes and toads.
All kinds of beasts and birds
are worshipped in this world.
I have seen owls leashed with chains,
and tiny creatures, buzzards and snakes, bred so small
they are kept in pockets,
sold plainly, at the market.

Birds or beasts or the shapes of men,
it does not matter what they worship. They invent
new organs, steal penises and lodge them
in birds' nests. They fuck each other day and night
with the angry faces of their gods.

They bring their children
before crowds and tell them
to wet their lips.

*

Beware if you think
you are guide dogs,
seeing eyes.
Each eye sees
a different world.
None is clearer.
None better lit.

You are whores
vomited from the sky.
From head to foot, each nucleus and membrane
longs for evil. When soldiers beat you,
when you are chased from your homeland,
trampled by teams of horses, rejoice!

It all depends on God.
He sits at His desk,
playing dominoes.
Some bones fall,
some stand.
Some are carved
and filled with perfumes,
others turned to ashtrays.
Each bone
solitary.

*

Wash your hands, give your worldly goods
to your enemies and file your taxes.
If God does not come soon,
I will,
after returning from Jerusalem.
We will turn Satan to grapes.
And you will dance on him
and drink him
like fine wine.

HURRY, SLOWLY

To hurry, slowly
through the world.
One eye on the heavens, another the unused bed.
Gliding urgently through Venice. Running
a business about intentions. It is
intentional. Dear God
I pray for the men with knotted wrists, for youths
with only paper in their pantries, for thick-fingered
scholars thumbing through chained libraries, their eyes
slowly, slowly
approaching darkness. And yet
I damn them, sending more and more
and more of these heavy letters
into the world, letters hidden
in extra folds but nonetheless
so heavy. Every part of me
aches with worry, and I fear the books,
if they are not to show losses, must fall further
into the vernacular. I can't think
how to anchor myself

if not with the Greeks. But without
a great deal of money, I cannot print. I sit
at Torresani's close dinner table, his tongue
moving, and me, an old man, dependent on
his sense of grasping. But no matter.
I can make every language
what it is destined to be: correct
and beautiful.

I am the same
as all scholars, we lean over lecturns,
presses, think
we need new shoes, but soon forget. We work
in the same small ocean of letters, at odds
with our accountants. I gather the remnants
of Constantinople in my house, where they argue
through whole editions, purge interpolations, correct
and restore proof, pour over manuscripts
sent from all Christendom. Until their eyes
gloss over. While armies, who cannot eat books,
who would wear book-leather on their feet, wrestle
each other, Musurus wrestles proof
stubborn as the hydra, errors propagating
faster than his pen can prune them. Would it
we could live on books alone,
we would spend years on each page. As it is
I fear I will be buried under leaves
of errata; gibberish will be
my purgatory, the devil,
composing stick in hand, yelling
a lash for each of life's mistakes.

I swim. There is no cheap
trick, no sudden ship or sea creature
to rescue me. Stroke by stroke I pull
nearer to antiquity. Forever nearer
but never arriving, never at rest
because *of making many books
there is no end, and much study
is a weariness of the flesh.* My flesh,

and each prince, each marchioness
crumbles. Rag paper, impressed
with me, remains.

LEAD

The presses hang heavy. The forest
envies them, and the letters. Their weight.
I want to buy a vowel,
but they're too rich for me. Vulnerable
to a toolbox of pliers and files,
but stubborn, stable, precise.
Thousands of miniature masterpieces
in lead. Spelling the world.

Words don't always rise to the surface.
Even though sidewalks repel,
chalk washes off. Sometimes
words punch right through.
I didn't think, I didn't wash my hands.
Look how many words I've eaten.

The Mad Hatter, Franklin's men, and me,
heavy headed, metal blooded.
Fuelled by what kills us, desire, delerium.
A murky end, beheaded, frozen,
when the letters become our oxygen,
and we drown.

LIBRARY

They looked like little pizzas
keeping warm inside
their cardboard boxes. But those were books
in the oven. Books in the pantry
too, pickled and canned, and cold,
frothy ones in the fridge. Books three deep
in the shelves, of course. Books before
and after dinner—aperitifs and sweets—
and books a bit drunk on the way out the door.
Emergency books in the trunk of the car.
Dirty ones lying on the backseat floor.

It was hard not to join them.
Tom Jones chased me 'round the dining room table
while *Pamela* locked herself in the china cabinet.
Sense and Sensibility raised an eyebrow. I had to pee
and there was *Moby-Dick* in the sink, pursuing the soap.
A drunken anthology of modernists was smoking in the living room.
Heart of Darkness crouched behind the bookends, waiting.

The Chaucer stayed in its shelf
and laughed and whispered
under its breath. The world, it said.
Sign here.

Room

Each morning, one half hour
of Proust. The window open, weather
bad. Warm under here. The women
silly, men fools, pages solid.
Has the rain stopped? Flowers
die on the sill, seeds fall
to my bed, folded in sheets, and after one
half hour, I rise, eat slowly, then if
it has stopped raining,
on my bike I bring
last night's letter to the boat.
I will not cross today. And so my letters,
and so my dear, dear reader.

Or else it keeps raining.
It falls and falls, plummets from the eavestrough
near the robin's nest, pools in the frost heaves
by the fire station, and I didn't bring my rain gear
here. Bike-chain
rusted. Splashguard gone.
My letters pile up, tacked
thick to corkboard.
My hand is big and takes so much
room. I'm afraid of running out.
But rain does not keep
the postman from the box. He takes the letters
onto the boat. Mine are missing.
I hoard them.

And I will not cross today,
and today, and today, and today.
I can't let my mind stray
to the city, you see. Dear reader,
I know you are there,
but you must share cities
with sidewalk spit and busy suited
pigeons on the go. All dead
set against us.
                    Here the air
is constructive and medicinal.
Someone feeds me. I have room
and read *À la recherche*
in random fragments. No
beginning, middle, end.

Don't make me cross.
I want to stay. Marcel has not finished
his tale. I'll come back
when my body gives in, and I have no more
letters in me.

Come on the next boat.
Pack a suitcase
of paper. Bring your own
hands and bike, rain pants,
bring a long novel, bring all
that I love.

ART AND ARTIFICE

You read Wordsworth. Then you wrote
a poem about friends, together, in a boat.
On an artificial lake I went canoeing, saw dead
goslings and gothic
bones seeping along with the mud from
a lakeside cemetery.

Spontaneous outpourings of emotion
aren't all they're cracked up to be. We sat wordless
too often, in a car, driving
stylish drags. In contemplation. Drunk.

We overdid it didn't we, friends aren't supposed
to let each other off, or confuse different shades
of "romantic."

Together we covered every movement. Parody
of literary history. You were an annoyingly
self-sufficient gentleman. Darcy
gone terribly wrong. Elizabeth
holding her tongue. We read too much
into ourselves.

You left me like a child's balloon, now a tiny red dot, then
gone, finally deflated, choking waterfowl on another continent.
Open-ended and silent. Forget closure. I miss you.

ALICE'S RIGHT FOOT

1.

Alice's Right Foot, Esquire.
So far away from her giant bony head
and flat Victorian pre-pubescence. A real
gentleman, uncomplaining, dreaming
his own dreams. But she knows it:
somewhere deep within tendons, the threat
to turn heel, stomp off
in the wrong direction, pulling her
body apart in the process like so much
treacle. Sometimes she feels
like he is already gone.

2.

Karen's left breast, on the other
hand. Immobilized
with duct tape, like a starlet's at the Oscars.
She is alone with her glamorous breast
until doors open, and middle-aged women
hover with questions.

Once so far away, Karen's left breast is now
in remarkable relief. Three, four, five dimensions
one being time but the fifth, the fifth is the dimension
where phantom limbs exist. Her breast has had only
a tiny peek there, but it is a place

not easily forgotten. It knows now
how to become a cratered science
fiction orb hurtling through dimensions pulling
her apart, her body spread
cold and thin as ultrasound lubricant.

And the little ball below the surface: it's called
a *breast mouse*. Because
it's slippery, won't sit still, slides around
under the microscope, runs off
with the gingerbread man. The breast giggles
like a class bully in the girls' locker room. Once a distant
drooping nuisance, the breast has won, is still
in remarkable relief. Relief
upon relief upon relief.

3.

Watch out for that girl over there, she might
have cancer. She first did it
when she was 18, these days she'll just disappear
for day surgery, return to work
a little tired. Don't let her fool you.

BUOYANCY

I will go down with my colours flying.

—VIRGINIA WOOLF

Crevices. The more you think,
the wider they open. Down
to monster air, to somewhere
they walk not on their feet
nor upside-down, on their hands,
but stomach down, rock
bottom, skulking in the hot rock sea.

You jump. Or are pushed. Or just
can't judge the distance.
Close your eyes and try
to balance on one foot,
and fall.
On all sides, shelves filled
with jars and bottles of all descriptions.
You smash
jam-jars as you fall, and eat
what you can grab, glass and all.

When you wake up, it's just before dawn,
you think, I should be sleeping,
is that burning the sun?
Either you go back to sleep,
face down in the molten sea,
or realize where you've fallen:

into the rumour of a gold mine.
You might blast
holes in your forehead.
No mirrors. No issue
of canaries at the door. You can drown
or not drown, but it's hard to tell
how long you've been down,
or which way is up.

And they may not want you, back up there.
Not with jam on your hands,
holes in your forehead, minerals cooling
over your skin. You are
dirty, stupid, frigid, and hopelessly
melodramatic. Best
immobilized in stone.

Those who drown
become the matrix. A stone soup
of bobbing bodies. Sometimes
arm after arm joins in a chain of arms,
reaching as high as it can to offer
swords and things,
to make you reach. And they pull you.
You grab what you can,
and reach the bottom, thinking,
it must be dawn, I should be
asleep—

*

If you go mining, sifting
stone through your fingers,
you have to hide your hands in your pockets and hope
they won't weigh you on your way out.
Down there, you gain and lose a lot of weight.

You need to find a geyser, be buoyant.
It might just be luck, you didn't want to leave,
you couldn't remember there's such a thing as up—
but it blasts you back to the surface.
Don't forget. You'll need that geyser
next time. Everyone's a suicide
bomber these days, fits happen
on every living-room floor, you'd think
we still believed in Freud,
in eating men like air, in crying.

Stay awake. There is an exit.
Sometimes you must leave
empty-handed. Remember.

THE YEAR I DID NOT READ

1.

The year I didn't read
musicians swam around my heels with vicious
tongues, magic swordfish.
Voices licked me,
words hit me but I was not
porous any more.

I wanted to be cheap,
lie back
and receive cold
images.

Sedate,
looking at books
from the outside, displaying them
in neat rows, weeding, watching
the colours of covers sway.

2.

I didn't read because
I could no longer unwind syntax, people
writing in circles. To trick me.
Sentences like
Porphyria's hair.
I dropped to the floor and when I woke

the books lay
closed in their shelves.

Libraries were contraband. I listened
to music all day, sent my stunt double
to school, and slept, and slept.
Poured sand
in my eyes and slowly stopped seeing
words scrolling across my lids' insides,
random, generated, a Scrabble jumble
hammered to a dream language,
nightmare gibberish, unedited, profane.

3.

The year I did not read, cats no longer sat in my lap, birds
sang only when trying to wake me.
Café strangers didn't smile.

But one day tangled strings of words
streamed from my eyes
and I could start again: A
for Apple, B for Baby, C for Cat.
Here comes the grinning kitty,
watching my lips move.
I start at the beginning,
looking over my shoulder
for the shadow readers
flicking their chains.

ON VISITING THE ALICE SHOP IN OXFORD

(and Telling the Shopkeeper about Another
Poem about Visiting the Alice Shop in Oxford)

I quit. Fled to England
from CanLit, to counter the lingering
thesis with its antithesis,
should it exist, some essential lack
of virgin wilderness and earnest
theoretical lesbians. I didn't find it, drifting
from museum to museum, marvelling
at colonial spoils and death masks
of Victorian poets. I rested

at the Alice Shop,
where the shopkeeper was busy
telling the story of the sheep and the barley sugar
to two Americans. Forever
I watched items remain still
in small bins, on hangers, sometimes behind glass.
A vague recollection. Did I buy something?
A cup and saucer, digestive biscuits, another book?

When the salesman finished his tale,
I told him about the poem
from a book of some renown, in my country,
a poem from home that spoke of exactly where I stood
that day. The salesman wished
I'd brought a copy, but I just stuttered,
couldn't remember the words.

Later, all I could do was pose
behind hedges. I had drowned
in a Ph.D. and was unmoved
by the Bodleian Library.

Oxford was such a lovely abstraction, I think,
and pour tea
in a cup where a cat smiles up
at me, drowning.

LEARNING TO GARDEN

All winter, no escape
from creaking floors, fields of white
linoleum. Winter was a black hole.
When I stepped out the door
in spring, everything made sense again.
Every memory worth having
happened outside.

All Mary Lennox needed
was the real English countryside.
How pink she glowed! By spring,
she was positively radioactive.

With just two months
of good weather, I did everything
outside: read
on the grass, tread
carefully between rows
of flowers. I wanted to know
why they were such military flowers,
stiff marigolds in rows and columns, mathematic.
(What I meant was: why can't we have an English garden?)
"Not in a row? You weed them then."
Mother was a little tired.

I wanted Mary to grow up
and marry Dickon, but they're always matched,
in these books, with their cousins,
which accounts for the lordly deformities.

Later in the story,
I will live in a house again
and have room. An ocean.
No telephone. A repertory cinema, and organic tropical fruit
at the market all winter, and trees all around me.

LOVE AND LOBLAW'S

In love and Loblaw's
nothing is fair.
But still they make us happy, as we
walk through the Garden Centre on St. Clair
smelling something green below
the smog. What do I know about gardening?
I make a big deal
of being a country girl,
but you've committed every leaf
to memory.

You told me your life story, saying
it would be the saddest story
I'd ever heard. You were right.
It clawed slowly up
the sides of your throat at night,
unused to the light entering
your lips. And still you walk contentedly
through Loblaw's Garden Centre, remembering,
while I weep—about what I don't even know.
The whole thing makes me feel a bit foolish
and weak, and write poems with begonias in them.

We should have Thanksgiving now, everyday.
Believe it! You deserve multitudes
of turkeys. I am grateful for the begonias,
even though they are so potted, and will vanish
from the sidewalk by September. I think I like
Toronto. I think this winter will be fine.

We're listening, heads
cocked to one side
(you and I and your birds).
They're your birds too,
you'd say. But that's not true,

not yet. This is close enough for now.
Look at you, looking at birds.
Your field guide says
a constellation of markings
in the shape of a "W"
has been said to portent War.
But bird, butterfly, or birthmark
could portent nothing but weather—
wind, maybe, and I
love wind. Coasting.

It's like this every day.
waking up after 7
or 17 or 27
years of sucking liquid
from the root of a tree, then flying around
whining like a chainsaw on speed:
mate mate mate mate mate mate mate mate mate!

Even for birds and bees it's not easy.
The perils of the food chain.
The wind feels so good
but changes my course.

I can't think with this buzzing
coming out of my throat!

Now it's raining and, if you're listening,
the rain always says the same thing.
You're all wet.
Go inside and take your clothes off.
I love rain.

THE ACCIDENTAL PRESS

I.

He brought me home
a press one day,
carried it on the subway,
carefully, in his arms,
plate just postcard
sized. Looking for chairs in a charity shop, he found it
unloved and unwanted, about to be
left curbside. He hid it
in the bed. I didn't notice it at first,
a very heavy pillow.

For months it sat
starting conversations. It doesn't work.
It misses parts. My hands are small, I can't help
carry it up the stairs.
I am slow to care for things.
Easily lulled, contented, forgetful.
We fight about it,

an object of weight
and maintenance. You can pull the handle
smooth as ice, but if one part's out of place:
nothing, or black mess.

2.

Scarborough General Hospital, 1972

Not long before we both are born, the press
falls out of use. They've hired a young new
therapist, a man with new-fangled ideas,
sick of the clinical space it fills, ink
all over. He knows newer ways
to occupy hands. The nurse
helps him roll the whole contraption
onto the elevator—the cabinet is a bugger
on the stairs—and stores it in the equipment
morgue. Poor press. Parts
falling off. A pad of charts
in the bottom drawer, little diagrams
of injured hands.

3.

I ride my bike across the bridge
to the mailbox on the other island.
Irresistible beach stones
fall into my pockets. I've been reading poems
where the lover dies. He was just like you.
I'm sad. The artists here talk
about art so much, and some of them are pregnant.

In Scarborough General Hospital right now,
some children are born, and some are not.
Some women fill their pockets
with stones and walk into lakes.
Some men's bicycles are mangled into scrap metal.
In the Occupational Therapy Clinic,
people are crying, and learning
to use their hands.

Some people bring babies
home on the subway, some people
bury their children.
Sometimes the same people;
sometimes people we love.

4.

I miss you and get caught in the rain
following birds off the path. You taught me birds.
Everywhere I look there are birds
where there were no birds before.

I remember the day you brought the press
home, resting carefully in your arms,
and I'm sorry I'm so slow, I'm so new,
I don't know how to take care of things,
or people, and I'm scared
of accidental presses falling
in my lap and growing.
If we miscalculate, if some element

is missing, there will be just
a pool of ink.

I would ask if you are going to stay.
But you wouldn't know; always,
deep in the works, something could be missing.
We can't tell yet. For now,
if I must have inky hands, I'd rather
you be the place
I leave my prints.

SALT AND BIRD

You can catch a bird by dashing
salt on its tail. You must be
quick, but not too quick,
not so quick you jerk the bird
into the sky and out
of the realm of the possible. The kids at school

say it can't be done but why
would your mother lie to you
about birds. Fluidity. Athleticism.
And your wits about you. Cunning.
Books can't teach you this.

The salt ineffable. One minute
you're heavy with it and the next the salt shaker
is empty and you can't remember seeing a single grain
fly through the air. You search and search
the ground and don't find any there.

You think you've gotten the bird once or twice,
The particular sparrow searching for stray
chicken-feed in the gravel. But you can't be sure:
the salt is invisible on its trajectory and, yes,
you must be mistaken.
It's flown away.

¶ I am grateful to those who worked on the book for Gaspereau Press: Clare Goulet, Kate Kennedy (the book's shepherd), Christina McRae & Andrew Steeves. For careful readings of individual poems, many thanks to Bert Almon, Shannon Bailey, Andrea Blundell, Dennis Cooley, Olga Costopoulos, Jennifer Dales, Jonathan Garfinkel, Shawna Lemay, Lindy Ledohowski, Jennifer LoveGrove, Tom Muir, Helen Stathopoulos, Annette Schouten Woudstra, and Deanna Young. For the title, Stephanie Shepherd and Miche Genest, who also gave a very helpful reading of the whole manuscript. Also thanks to Silas White and Carleton Wilson for their comments. Thanks for the tour of Crispin and Jan Elsted's Barbarian Press, arranged by Jillian Shoichet. For time and space, thanks to Toronto Artscape, the Gibraltar Point Artists' Residency Program, Susan Serran, the Sage Hill Writing Experience, St. Michael's Retreat, the Friends of Poetry, and Steven Ross Smith. For financial support, the Alberta Foundation for the Arts, the Ontario Arts Council, and the Canada Council for the Arts.

Some of these poems, often in earlier forms, have appeared in The Danforth Review (on-line), the above/ground press chapbook FLAME, Grain, Jacket (on-line from Australia), LRC: The Literary Review of Canada, The New Quarterly, Taddle Creek, and the Wood Tick Press chapbook Two Roosters Three Dragons and a Tiger. Many thanks to the editors, especially Erin Bow, Michael Bryson, Lesley Elliott, Kim Jernigan, and rob mclennan.

The books are too numerous to list, but I am particularly indebted to Lewis Carroll's Alice in Wonderland and Alice Through the Looking Glass, Lucy Maud Montgomery's Anne of Green Gables, Charlotte Brontë's Jane Eyre, and Kristjana Gunnars's The Rose Garden: Reading Marcel Proust.

My love and thanks to my most dear reader, Adam Levin. I've said this before. You + the books = joy.

THREE ROSE GARDEN VARIATIONS The italicized quotations at the beginning of each poem are from Kristjana Gunnars's book *The Rose Garden: Reading Marcel Proust* (Red Deer Press, 1997).

JOANNA Joanna is a typeface by Eric Gill (d. 1940), British stonecutter, illustrator, sculptor, and type designer. Gill was a fanatical and eccentric Catholic who lived with extended family and hangers-on in patriarchal back-to-the-land communes, and who had a voracious, unconventional, and disturbing sexual appetite which included, among other things, incestuous relationships with his sisters and his daughters. Gill's works include the sculpture *Prospero and Ariel* for the BBC building, and a rather scandalously illustrated edition of the Song of Songs for Golden Cockerel Press. The quotations at the beginning and ending of the poem are from the Song of Songs.

HURRY, SLOWLY Venetian printer Aldus Manutius (d. 1516) is considered by many to be the greatest printer and publisher in history. His colophon was the dolphin and anchor, and his motto *Festina Lente*. He is credited with popularizing italic type and the quarto-sized book. He eventually married the daughter of his financial backer, Torresani. Aldus specialized in scholarly Greek texts; Musurus was his chief Greek editor. I had the opportunity to view some of the Wosk-Macdonald Aldine Collection at the Simon Fraser University Library in the spring of 2000. The quotation in italics is from Ecclesiastes.

ON VISITING THE ALICE SHOP IN OXFORD The poem mentioned is Stephanie Bolster's "Visitor from Overseas, Reprise" in her book *White Stone: The Alice Poems*.

Typeset in Agfa Monotype's digital interpretation of
Eric Gill's Joanna by Andrew Steeves & printed offset
at Gaspereau Press on Zephyr Antique Laid paper.

Gaspereau Press acknowledges the support of
the Canada Council for the Arts & the Nova Scotia
Department of Tourism and Culture.

2   4   6   8   9   7   5   3   1

National Library of Canada Cataloguing In Publication

Press, Karen, 1974–
Spine / K.I. Press.

Poems.
ISBN 1-894031-90-3

I. Title.

PS8581.R39S64 2004
C811'.6   C2004-902117-6

GASPEREAU PRESS ¶ PRINTERS & PUBLISHERS
ONE CHURCH AVENUE, KENTVILLE, NOVA SCOTIA
CANADA B4N 2M7